Table of Contents

Preface

Pakshaghata, as described in Ayurvedic classics, is a complex and debilitating manifestation of aggravated Vata dosha, often correlated with hemiplegia in modern medical science. It is not merely a disease of motor dysfunction but a challenge to one's independence, mobility, and overall quality of life. With its increasing incidence, especially in geriatric and lifestyle-related contexts, the need for a holistic and integrative approach to treatment has never been more crucial.

This book, "Elucidating Pakshaghata: An Ayurvedic Approach to Hemiplegia", is an effort to systematically explore the etiology, pathogenesis, clinical presentation, and comprehensive Ayurvedic management of Pakshaghata, supported by classical references, clinical protocols, and current research insights.

Drawing upon authoritative sources such as Charaka Samhita, Ashtanga Hridaya, and Sushruta Samhita, as well as contemporary clinical experience, the chapters delve into the disease's samprapti (pathogenesis), chikitsa siddhanta (treatment principles), and therapeutic measures such as Panchakarma, Rasayana, Shamana, and external therapies. Special emphasis is given to the integration of physiotherapy, diet, Yoga, and modern neurorehabilitation, reflecting the scope of Ayurveda in today's healthcare framework.

This work is intended to serve as a practical and theoretical guide for Ayurvedic students, practitioners, researchers, and healthcare professionals who are engaged in treating neuromuscular and neurovascular conditions. It may also benefit those seeking a deeper understanding of how ancient wisdom can address modern neurological disorders with compassion, precision, and scientific grounding.

I sincerely hope that this book becomes a valuable companion in clinical practice and academic study, encouraging further exploration and documentation of Ayurvedic approaches to complex conditions like Pakshaghata.

With humility and dedication,

Dr. Asharani R Medidar

BAMS, MD

Acknowledgement

I express my sincere gratitude to my teachers and mentors for their invaluable guidance and encouragement throughout the preparation of this book.

My heartfelt thanks to the patients who entrusted me with their care and inspired this work through their healing journeys.

I am deeply thankful to my family and friends for their constant support and patience.

Finally, I bow to the ancient Ayurvedic texts and sages whose timeless wisdom forms the foundation of this study.

Pakshaghata has been derived from "Pakshyasya Aghata iti Pakshaghata". The word Pakshaghata is composed of two Sanskrit words i.e. Paksha + Aghata. The individual meaning of these words is as follows –

Paksha:

- According to Vachaspathyam – Paksha + Aghata i.e. Parshva matre – means side
- According to Shabdakalpadrum – Parshvamatram – means Parshva means dehanga.
- According to Shabdasthom mahanidhi – Parshwa means side. Dehardha means half of the body.
    - Paksha - Dehangam = Part
    - Paksha - Parshva = Flank or side
    - Paksha-Dehardha =Half of body
    - Paksha-Dehanga bheda = Member of body
- Acharya Sushrutha while explaining about Pakshaghata has used the word "Paksha" Dalhana commented on this by saying it as "Shareerardham".
- Ashtanga sangraha and Ashtanga Hridaya also used the word "Paksha" which gives the same meaning as mentioned by Sushrutha. Vijayarakshita, commentator of Madhava nidana explains the meaning of "Paksha" as "Ardhanarishwaravat"

- Sharangadhara Samhita, Bhavaprakasha, Yogaratnakara have used the word Paksha with the meaning as half of the body. From the above it implies that the word Paksha refers to one side of body.

Aghata:

The word Aghata is derived from the word "An+Han+Ghan"

"Han+Vich+Bhave+Lyut"

The word Aghata depicts different meanings. Some are as follows Aghata=Vadha = Killing

- Aghata=Hanana = Destruction
- From the Aghata =Prahara = A Blow

Putting all these meaning together, the word Ghata means Killing, Blow, and Injury

In Ayurveda the word Ghata have been quoted in various contexts like Marmaghata, Mutraghata etc. It shows reduced activities.

- Vadha – to kill; Prahara –to kill with a blow.

VADHA- to Kill

From the above description it shows that Ghata and Vadha have similar meaning. So also, Pakshaghata and Pakshavadha are having same meaning. Based on the meaning of the individual term paksha, vadha and aghata the word pakshaghata is derived as under.

Pakshaghata: According to Shabdhakalpadruma Pakshaghata has been defined as – "Pakshaghata Dehangasya Ghatam Vinashanam Yasmat Yatra va"

It means loss of function of one side of the body. Sir Williams confined the meaning of Pakshaghata to stroke or hemiplegia only.

Definition of Hemiplegia

The term hemiplegia is derived from a compound Greek word. Here hemi means half and plegia means paralysis or stroke. Therefore, hemiplegia can be defined as a clinical feature of one side weakness or paralysis in upper and lower extremities and a part of face. Hemiplegia is the commonest manifestation of a stroke with a paralysis effect on the face, limbs and trunk or one side of the body.

Stroke

Synonyms – Apoplexy, Cerebrovascular Accidents.

The term stroke is defined as a rapid onset of focal neurological deficit, over minutes or hours resulting from the diseases of the cerebral vasculature and its contents.

Paralysis

It is derived from the words – 'para' – besides, beyond; and 'lysis' – breaking up or death. Paralysis is loss of voluntary movement due to interruption of motor pathway at any point from the cerebrum to the muscle fiber. Summing up, Hemiplegia means paralysis of one half of the body affecting both arm and leg and sometimes face.

Historical Review

Vedas are considered to be the oldest epics of the world. Scattered references of Vata Dosha and disorders related to Vata are found in Vedas. Five types of Vata have been listed in Atharvaveda, namely; Praana, Apana, Vyana, Samana, and Udana. (A.V.10.2:13). Pippali (A.V. 6.109:3) and Vashanaka (A.V.6.44:33) two drugs have been mentioned in Atharvaveda which have been claimed as 'Vatakritasya Bheshaja' and 'Vatakrita Naasani' respectively. Blumefield interprets the word Vatakrita as the disorder caused by Vata. Pakshaghata and Pakshavadha are not mentioned in Vedas but Angabheda (A.V.9.13.1:22) mentioned in Atharvaveda and Pangu (R.V.2.15:7) mentioned in Rigveda indicates the knowledge regarding the Pakshaghata related diseases in that era.

Upanishad:

In Prashaopanishad – Gati of Udana Vayu and Importance of Vyana vayu are mentioned.

In Ramayana – Importance of Vayu has been discussed in relation to health.

In Garuda purana – Various vata prakopa nidanas have been explained

In Vishnu purana – Various gunas of vayu have been mentioned.

Detailed description regarding Pakshaghata has been mentioned by the Acharya in the Samhitas.

CHARAKA SAMHITA: (1000 BC- 2nd AD)

Pakshavadha and Pakshagraha are considered Madhyama Roga Maargaja vyadhi, i.e., Marm-Asthi-Sandhi Maarga (Ch. Su.11/49). Pakshavadha considered one among eighty Naanaatmaja Vaata Vikaaras (Ch.Su. 20/11) and detailed description of the disease has been given as Pakshavadha (Ch. Chi. 28/53, 54). Achaarya Charaka has given the line of treatment as "Swedanam Sneha Samyuktam Pakshaghate Virechanam". Jejjata (9th Cen.) clarifies this by saying that Swedana and Virechana should be administered along with Sneha in pakshagata. Gangadhara (19th Cen.) comments that Snehayukta Swedana and Snehayukta Virechana should be given in Pakshaghata.

Bhela and Harita Samhita (1000 BC- 2nd cent.AD)

Only a brief description of Pakshaghata is available in both these Samhitas. In third Sthana of Harita Samhita 20th Chapter some information regarding diseases related to Pakshaghata namely EkangaVaata and Ekanga Pakshaghata is available.

SUSHRUTA SAMHITA: (2nd cent. A.D)

Etiopathogeneses, clinical features and prognosis of Pakshaghata have been described in the first chapter of Nidaana Sthana. The role of Urdhvagaami, Adhogami, and Tiryaga

Dhamanis in the pathogenesis of Pakshaghata has been explained. Lakshana, Anyatara Pakshahanana, Sandhi Bandhana Vimoksha has been added here. In Mahavata Vyadhi adhyaya of Chikitsa Sthana (Su. Chi. 5/19) treatment of Pakshaghata has been described. Vata Vyaadhi has highlighted among Ashta Mahagada in Sh.Su. 33. Akarmanyata as Ishatkarmakshayam - partial loss of function, where patient is unable to maintain stance and tends to fall has interpreted by commentator Dalhana. He interprets Achetana as Alpachetana, referring to partial loss of sensation.

Sangraha kala (100AD-800AD):

Ashtang Sangraha And Ashtang Hridaya: (2-6th cent. AD)
Similar description of Pakshaghata is found in both these Samhita. In Ashtaanga Samgraha, the general Nidana of Vata Vyadhi, signs, symptoms and prognosis of Pakshaghata has been given in 15th chapter of Nidana Sthana. The treatment has been highlighted in Chikitsa Sthana, 23rd chapter.

Pakshaghata has been described in Ashtanga Hridaya 15th chapter of Nidana Sthana and 21st chapter of Chikitsa Sthana. The term Anyatara Paksha Nasha has been used here and commentator Arundatta (11th Cen.) interprets word Anyatara as right or left side of the body. Line of treatment is same as that given by Charaka with the only difference that Sneha is mentioned instead of Swedana.

Kashyapa samhita:

In this Samhita Pakshaghata has been listed among 80 types of Nanatmaja Vata Vyadhi (K.S. Su. 27-28). It is also included in the list of Swedana arha (K.S. Su. 23-22). More details of Pakshaghata are not found in the available edition of this Samhita.

Madhav nidaana: (7th cent. AD)

Pakshaghata has been described in detail here. General description of causative factors, pathogenesis, signs and symptoms of all Vaata Vyaadhi is found in 22nd chapter. In addition to the general symptoms of Pakshaghata, Pitta and Kapha Anubandha Lakshana have also been described. Commentator Vijaya Rakshita (14th Cen.) has differentiated Pakshaghata from Adharaanga Vaata by giving illustration of 'Ardhanaarishwaravat' to the former and 'Narsimhavat' to the latter.

Nyaaya chandrikaa:

Gayadas has been interpreted the Lakshana "Sandhibandha Vimoksham" as "Sandhibandhaan Kaphasanhitaabhih Dhamanibhih Kritan Mokshayan Pakshaghatam Kuryaat."

Chakradatta(12th cent. AD)

Detailed description of Vatavyadhi Chikitsa has been described in 22nd chapter. For the treatment of Pakshaghata some formulations are indicated.

14

Vangasena Samhita (12th cent. AD)

In Vatavyadhyi-Adhikara a detailed desription of Pakshaghata is explained with its pathogenesis, prognosis and symptomatology. The line of treatment given here Snehana, Swedana and Virechana.

Sharangadhara Samhita (13th cent. AD)

In Purvakhanda of Sharangadhara samhita had enumerated Pakshaghata among the 80- Vata Nanatmaja disorders (7/107). In Madhyamakhanda 2/92; and 2/142 some formulations for Pakshaghata are mentioned.

Bhavaprakasha (15th cent. AD)

Detailed description of pakshagat is present in Bhava.Prakash. M. 24/205-207, 262,263.

Yogaratnakara (17th cent. AD)

Description of Vatavyadhi similar to that of Madhava Nidana is found in the Nidana chapter. Some specific treatments are indicated for Pakshaghata.

Bhaishajya Ratnavali (18th cent. AD)

In the 26th chapter named as Vata Vyadhi Chikitsa detailed description of Chikitsa of Vatavyadhi is present. For Pakshaghata some drug formulations are also indicated. Other treatises i.e in Kalyanakaraka of Ugradityacharya(9th Cent.), Chikitsakalika by

Hippocrates (400 B.C.): He observed that there were many blood vessels connected to the brain. He notified the most significant fact regarding Hemiplegia, that "If the patient has the lesion of the left side of the head, spasm seizes the right side of the body; if the lesion is on the right side of the head; spasm seizes the left side of the body."

Galen (131-201A.D.): described the anatomy of the brain and its blood vessels.

The 16th century is truly designated as the age of Anatomy.

Andreas Vesalius (1541-1564) produced sketches of brain, nerves, etc., after extensive experimental studies.

The 17th century is known as century of physiology. Several discoveries took place in this century.

William Harvey (1578-1657 A.D.) described the circulation of blood.

In 18th century the focus attention was shifted to pathology and the cause of disease

Giovanni Battista Morgagni (1682-1771) is a father of Pathology described one case of hemiplegia. He recognized that paralysis was on the side of the body opposite to the brain lesion.

19th century gave rise to many discoveries, new theories and emergence of modern medicine.

John Cheyne (1777-1836) described the morbid appearance of patient's brain and neurological abnormalities in detail.

Fisher termed the temporary short-lived episodes of neurological symptoms as Transient Ischemic Attacks (TIAs).

In 20th century progress in medical science geared up.

The work of British physiologist-**Charles Scott Sherrington** on nervous system led to the better understanding of nervous diseases including Hemiplegia. He assigned the functions of co-ordination to the nervous system, studied the levels of nervous integration, the proprioceptive system, the higher controlling centres and central inhibitors. Today, there is a wealth of information available on the cause, prevention, risk, and management of stroke. However, in spite of all this information and breakthroughs there is no any confirming treatment to reduce the risk of death and disability.

Classification Of Pakshaghata:

Aacharya Sushruta while describing the prognosis of Pakshaghatahas classified the disease in three types as per their aetiopathogenesis.

The three types of Pakshaghata are as follows:

1. Suddha Vaataja Pakshaghata:- where the Vata is aggravated on account of its own Nidaana
2. Anyadosha Samsrista Pakshaghata: - where the Vata is associated with other Dosha to manifest the disease.
3. Kshaya Hetuja Pakshaghata: - where the Vata is aggravated as a consequence of Dhatu Kshaya.

Acharya Sushruta has used the terms Samanvita, Samsrista, Anvita, Samyukta etc as synonym of Avarana in the context of description of Avarana.

The routes of Vata Prakopa are:

1. Svanidanjanya Vata Prakopa: Due to indulgence in its own Nidana the Vata gets provocated.
2. Margavaranajanya Vata Prakopa: The normal functions of Vata depend on three factors viz. Avyahata Gati, Vata to be seated at its own natural site, Vata to be remains in its normal quality. When there is obstruction of the path of the Vayu by another Dosha or Dushya, the Avyahata Gati of Vata is hampered and Vayu get

provocated. This type of vitiation of Vata is called Margavaranajanya Vata Prakopa.

3. Dhatu Kshaya Janya Vata Prakopa: When there is Dhatu Kshaya, there develops some vacum in the Dhatu which get filled by Vayu and the Vata get provocated. This type of Vata Prakopa is called Dhatu Kshaya Janya Vata Prakopa. Svanidanajanya Vata Prakopa results in the manifestation of Suddha Vataja Pakshaghata. Margavarana Janya Vata Prakopa results in the manifestation of Anya Dosha Samsrista Pakshaghata and Dhatu Kshaya Janya Vata Prakopa results in ksaya hetuja Pakshaghata. The Dhatukshayajanya Pakshaghata as again classified as

Acharya Gaydas as,

1. Sonitaatisritikrita Dhatu Kshaya Janya Pakshaghata and

2. Balavadvigrahadita Dhatu Kshaya Janya Pakshaghata.

Classification as per causes of hemiplegia:

Sudden Onset Hemiplegia:

- Cerebrovascular Accident
- Intracranial infection - Encephalitis, meningitis, congestive attacks of GPI
- Trauma - Depressed fracture of skull

- Todd's paralysis (Post ictal)
- Hysterical

Gradual Onset Hemiplegia:

- Cerebral Tumor
- Chronic subdural hematoma
- Infections - cerebral abscess, meningitis and encephalitis
- General paralysis of insane
- Congenital defects - cerebral agenesis

Transient Or Recurrent Hemiplegia:

- Transient ischemic attacks
- Hypertensive encephalopathy
- Post epileptic
- Congestive attack of GPI
- Hysterical
- Multiple sclerosis
- Hemiplegic migraine

Hemiplegia caused by each of the above disease has got different aetiopathogenesis and line of management. All the above causes of hemiplegia can be categorized under the three groups of Pakshaghata considering their nature of disease process and etiopathogenesis. But this requires a thorough study of each of above disease in term of Nidana Panchaka to determine their Samprapti in terms of Ayurveda.

Synonyms

Synonyms

In Ayurveda different paryayas or synonyms has been used to denote the disease process, avayava, etiology, pathology, etc. Pakshaghata, Pakshavadha, Ardhangavata, Pakshagraha, Ekanga vata, Pakshahata, etc.

Nidana

The word Nidana bears two meanings; one is causative factor and other is diagnosis. Nidana may be dosha aggravating, disease aggravating or aggravating both. It may also be classified as a general one and specific one. The importance of Nidana in the management of any disease can be well understood from the verse. To understand various nidana, each can be classified systematically under four categories.

1) Aharajanya, 2) Viharajanya, 3) Manasa and 4) Anya. Nidana described in various Ayurvedic texts are as below:

Charaka Samhita: In Charaka Samhita, specific nidana of Pakshaghata are not described. General Nidana of Vatavyadhi can be taken as a token for Pakshaghata also. The nidana mentioned in Ch. Chi. 28 are as under.

Aharajanya: Excessive intake of annadravya which are Ruksha, Shita, Laghu in Guna, Alpa Anna Sevana, Langhana and Ama. Here Vijayrakshita says that Ama causes Prakopa by Avarana.

Viharajanya: Ativyavaya, Atiprajagarana, Atiplavana, Ativyayama, Dukhashaiyya, Dukhasana, Divaswapna, Vegadharana and Atiadhva.

Manasa: Atichinta, Shoka, Krodha and Bhaya.

Agantuja: Abhighata, Marmaghata, Gaja apatamsana, Ushtra aptamsana, Ashwa apatamsana and shigra Yana apatamsana. Here Vijayrakshita gives one more meaning of the word 'Apatamsana'. He says that besides 'Patanam' and 'Dhatuksharana' it also means 'Ucchvasarodha' i.e. difficulty in inspiration caused by riding on elephant, camel, horse or another fast vehicle.

Miscellaneous: Vishama Upachara, Dosha Atisravana, Asruka Atisravana, Dhatu Sankshaya, Rogatikarshana and Riktasrotasa are other nidana of vatavyadhi.

Table No-1 - Aharaja Nidana:

Etiological Factors	Ch.	Su	A.S	A.H	Bh.P
Alpa/Pramita Anna	+	-	+	+	+
Laghu Anna	+	-	+	-	+
Langhana	+	-	-	-	-
Abhojana/Anashana	+	+	-	-	+
Vishamaashana	-	+	-	-	+
Adhyashana	-	+	-	-	-
Vishtambhi	-	-	-	-	-
Shushka Shaaka	-	+	-	-	-
Vallura (Shushka Maamsa)	-	+	-	-	-
Varaka(Kudhaanya)	-	+	-	-	-

Uddaalaka	-	+	-	-	+
Koradusha	-	+	-	-	-
Shyaamaaka	-	+	-	-	+
Nivaara	-	+	-	-	+
Mudga	-	+	-	-	+
Masura	-	+	-	-	+
Aadhaki	-	+	-	-	+
Harenukaa (Kalaaya Bheda)	-	+	-	-	-
Nishpaava	-	+	-	-	+
Kalaaya	-	+	+	-	-
Khesari (Triput)	-	-	+	-	+
Chanaka	-	-	+	-	+
Makushtha	-	-	-	-	+
Varati	-	-	-	-	+
Mangalya (Masura Bheda)	-	-	-	-	+
Satina (Kalaaya Bheda)	-	-	-	-	+
Bhukte hi Ajeerneh Ashanam	-	-	-	-	+
Bisa, Shaaluka, Tinduka	-	-	+	-	-
Karira, Kaalinga, Jaambava	-	-	+	-	-

Table No-2 - **Viharaja Nidana:**

Nidanas	Ch.		Su	A.S.	A.H.	Bh.P
Ati Vyavaaya	+		+	+	+	+
Ati Prajaagaran	+		+	+	+	+
Langhana	+		+	+	-	+
Plavana	+		+	-	-	-
Pratarana	-		+	+	-	+
Atiadhva	+		-	+	-	-
Ati Vyaayaama	+		+	+	+	-
Ativicheshtaa	+		-	-	-	-
Dukhashayya	+		-	-	-	-
Dukha-Aasana	+		-	-	-	-
Divaaswapna	+		-	-	-	-
Atiadhyayana	-		+	+	-	-
Pradhaavana	+		-	+	-	-
Bhaaraharana	-		+	-	-	-
Vegasandhaarana	+		+	+	+	+
Uchchabhaashana	-		-	+	+	-
Gajaaticharyaa	-		+	+	-	-
Turangaaticharyaa	-		+	-	-	-

Ratha-Aticharyaa	-		+	-	-	-
Pada Aticharyaa	-		+	-	-	-
Yaan (Ati Savaari)	-		-	-	-	-
Shaityataa	-		-	-	-	+
Ati Shrama	-		-	-	-	+
Gadhochchadana	-		-	+	-	-
Trushitaasana	-		-	+	-	-
Kshudhitambupana	-		-	+	-	-

Table No-3 - **Aghataja Nidana:**

Aetiological Factors	Ch.	Su.	A.S.	A.H.	Bh.P.
Abhighaata	+	+	+	-	+
Marmaaghaata	+	-	-	-	-
Balvad Vigraha	-	+	+	-	-
Prapatan – Gaj, Ushtra, Ashva, Yaan, Tara (Tree), Atiuccha Patanam	+	+	-	-	+
Prapidana / Prahaara (Dandaadi)	-	+	-	-	-
Ashma / Shila / Loha / Kashtha – Utkshepa, Vikshepa, Bhramana, Chalana	-	-	+	-	-

Marmaghata:

Shiromarmaghata leads to Ardita, Spandana, Svarahani, Cheshtanasha, Mukatva etc Trauma to Lohitaksha Marma leads to excessive blood loss, Pakshavadha and even death. Due to Doshaja Aghata on this Marma, Sira and Snayu Shosha takes place, this leads to Pakshavadha.

Same principle is applicable where Sushruta mentioned Pakshaghata as a Vranopradrava. Pakshaghata is a consequence of Kakshadhara Marmaghata. This is because of Snayu are intensively involved in this Marmaghata.

Manasika Nidana:

Table No-4

Aetiological Factors	Ch.	Su.	A.S.	A.H.	Bh.P
Chintaa	+	-	-	+	+
Shoka	+	-	+	+	+
Krodha	+	-	-	-	-
Bhaya	+	-	-	+	+
Kaama	+	-	-	-	+
Apravritta Vegodirana	-	-	+	+	-
Utkanthaa	-	-	+	-	-

Kalaja Nidana:

Table No-5

Pravaata	-	+	-	-	-
Grishma Ante	-	-	+	+	-
Jeerna Ante	-	+	-	-	-
Ahoratri Ante	-	-	+	+	+
Shishir Ritu	-	-	-	-	+
Varshaa Ritu	-	+	+	-	+
Pradoshe	-	-	-	-	-
Bhukta Ante	-	-	-	+	-
Shita Kaala	-	+	-	-	-
Abhra	-	+	-	-	-
Prabhaata Kaala	-	+	-	-	-
Aparaahna	-	+	+	-	-
Himam	-	-	-	-	+
PraagVaata	-	-	+	-	+

Causes Of Cerebrovascular Accident:

Stroke is the clinical term for acute loss of circulation to an area of the brain, resulting in ischemia and a corresponding loss of neurologic function. Classified as either hemorrhagic or ischemic, strokes typically manifest with the sudden onset of focal neurologic deficits, such as weakness, sensory deficit, or difficulties with language. Ischemic strokes have a heterogeneous group of causes, including thrombosis, embolism, and hypo perfusion, whereas hemorrhagic strokes can be either intraparenchymal or subarachnoid. The lists of causes of different groups of strokes are as follows.

Causes of thrombotic stroke:

- Arterial: -Atherosclerosis, arteritis, syphilis, collagen diseases
- Venous: -Cortical thrombophlebitis, postpartum or post   operative thrombophlebitis

Presentation- Pakshaghata explained by Acharya Caraka can be considered under Thrombotic Stroke

- The onset of thrombotic stroke is sudden and progressive (i.e Stepwise evolution)
- Incidence is high during sleep and it affects usually elderly
- Usually there is preservation of consciousness
- No seizure or headache

- There is gradual recovery
- Usually there is evidence of atherosclerosis

Causes of embolic stroke: - Embolisms are usually from,

- Heart: - Auricular fibrillation, myocardial infarction, infective endocarditis
- Arteries: - Detachment of an atheromatous plaque usually from the aorta or the carotid artery
- Veins: - Thrombophlebitis usually from the veins of lower limb and pelvis
- Miscellaneous: - Post cardiac surgery, caisson's disease

The Complete Stroke explained by Acharya Sushruta can be considered under Hemorrhagic and embolic Stroke

Presentation-

- Abrupt development of completed stroke within few seconds
- Rapid partial improvement within minutes or hours
- Occurs at any age and time of the day
- Relative preservation of consciousness
- There might be evidence of recent stroke

Causes of hemorrhagic stroke: - Hemorrhage are usually from the rupture of

- Berry's aneurisms

- Atherosclerotic vessel
- Angiomatous malformation
- Hypertensive encephalopathy

Presentation-

- Presence of hypertension(known/undetected)
- Catastrophic onset
- Onset during waking hours-usually
- Headache, seizures, vomiting are present
- Deepening Stupor/coma
- Gradually progressive symptoms
- Nuchal rigidity
- Delayed or no recovery

Based on Clinical presentation hemiplegia can be understood in fallowing ways-

- **Transient Ischemic Attack**- Is an acute focal neurological deficit resulting from cerebrovascular disease with resolution of signs and symptoms within 24 hours.
- **Reversible Ischemic Neurological deficit (RIND)-** Attack lasting longer than 24 hours with complete clearance of signs and symptoms within 7 days
- **Complete stroke-** Neurological deficit lasts longer trhan 7 days with or without partial recovery.

Risk Factors of Stroke:

Irreversible risk factors

- Age
- Sex (Male are more effected than female except in very young and very old)
- Race (Afro-Caribbean > Asian >European)
- Hereditary

Modifiable risk factors

- Hypertension
- Heart disease (heart failure, atrial fibrillation)
- Diabetes mellitus
- Hyperlipidemia
- Obesity
- Smoking
- Excess alcohol consumption
- Polycythemia
- Oral contraceptive

The Purvarupa for Pakshaaghata in particular has not been described in Ayurvedic text. However, purvarupa of vaata vyaadhi in general has been described by Aachaarya Charaka by saying that Avyakta Lakshana is the Purva Rupa of any vaata vyaadhi. Here, Chakrapani has commented that Avyakta means few or mild symptoms and Gangadhara has also opined the same. Vijayarakshita has thrown more light on the word Avyakta and says that the symptoms that are not manifested clearly are Purva Rupa and these are due to –Less severity of causative factors, Few or mild symptoms, Less Aavarana of Dosha

Purvarupa usually manifest due to the Sthaanasamsraya of Dosha at the time of Dosha Dushya Sammurchchhanaa. Purvarupa will be more manifest when the Dosha get provocated through usual route of Sanchaya, Prakopa and Prasara. This type of provocation is found in Swanidaanajanya or Suddha Vaataja Pakshaghata. But in case of Aavaranajanya the Vaayu is not get provocated through the route of Sanchaya, Prakopa etc. rather the Vaayu get provocated suddenly due to Aavarana so Purvarupa are not found in Aavaranajanya Pakshaghaata.

Prodromal Symptoms of Stroke:

Prodromal symptoms are not found in stroke resulting from embolism and hemorrhage. In this case the stroke manifests suddenly. But the stroke resulting from thrombosis sometimes may show prodromal symptoms like, difficulty in speaking, weakness of arm or leg, vertigo may be present.

The symptoms which evolve or are manifested in Vyakta Avasthaa of Shadvidha kriyaakala are known as Rupa. Various symptoms of Pakshaghata described in Ayurvedic literature are as follows:

Charaka Samhita:

The signs and symptoms of Pakshaghata as described by Aacharya Charaka are Vama or Dakshina Pakshahanana along with-

- Cheshtaanivriti: Loss of voluntary movements, which is the cardinal symptom of this disease.
- Ruja: Pain
- Vaakstambha : Aphasia or Dysarthria
- Padam sankochayakam hastam- Spasticity in limbs
- Todshulakrut- Sensory Symptoms(vague pain)

Sushruta Samhita:

In Sushruta Samhita the symptoms of Pakshaaghaata are described as follows,

- Anyatara Pakshahanana
- Sandhi Bandha Vimoksha
- Akarmanyataa
- Acetanam (loss of sensation or consciousness)

Here, Sandhi Bandha Vimoksha and Anyatara Pakshahanana are described for the first time

Ashtaanga Samgraha and Hridaya:

Vagbhata has followed Sushruta in describing the symptomatology of Pakshaghata (A.S. Ni. 15/40-42).

Maadhava Nidaana: In this text also the description of the clinical picture of Pakshaghata is of the same opinion with that of Sushruta and Vagbhata. In Maadhava Nidana in addition to general symptoms of Pakshaghata the Pittaanuvandha and Kaphaanuvandha Lakshana of Pakshaghata are also described. Pittaanuvandha Pakshaghata is characterized by Daha, Murchchha, and Santapa. Kaphanubandhi Pakshaghata is characterized by Shotha, Gaurava and Stambha.

Sushruta and Vaagbhata have considered the word 'Ekaanga Roga' as synonym of Pakshaghata.

Bhavaprakasha: Bhavaprakasha has literally followed Maadhava Nidaana, while describing Pakshaghata.

Cranial nerve involvement and their manifestations are explained by acharya Caraka and Vagbhata in the context of Ardita and Pakshaghata as fallows -one should thoroughly examine and analyze the patient of pakshaghata

1. Olfactory Nerve- Gandhajnana

2. Optic- Netradeenam ch vaikrutim

3. Oculomotor-

4. Abducent- vaikrutam   Strhabdha Netra, Netradenam ch

6. Trochlear-

5. Trigemenal-   Vakrikaroti hanu/Shankha/Sravana/Gandhaha ruk

7. Facial- Vakrikaroti nasa, bhru, lalata/Mukham Jinham/Vrujati asye Bhojana/Bhidyate swra/Kshavathu Nigraha

8. Vestibulo-cochlear- Badyate Sewaram

9. Glossopharyngeal-   Mukham Jinham

10. Vagus

11. Spinal Accessory- Upashosha bahum

12. Hypoglossal-Mukham Jinham

The signs and symptoms of stroke depend upon the following factors.

- Nature of vascular lesion
- Duration of ischemia
- Region of the brain supplied by the Affected vessel
- Status of the collaterals to that region
- Vulnerability of neurons of that region

The process starting right from the vitiation of the dosha to the complete manifestation of the disease is known as Samprapti. Each and every step from a healthy state to a   diseased one are included in Samprapti. Knowledge of Samprapti is inevitable for Vaidya, because blockage of the pathogenesis at any of the stage will terminate the disease, thereby preventing the mortality and morbidity.Again it should be bared in mind that different regimens are to be applied at different stages. Conventionally the Samprapti can be of two types.

General or Samanya Samprapti: This is a common pathogenesis among various types of a single disease.

Specific or Vishishta Samprapti: This is a specific pathogenesis for a particular subtype.

Samanya Samprapti of Pakshaghata: This is the general samprapti of pakshaghata common for all vatavyadhi. The samanya samprapti of pakshaghata according to Charaka Samhita is as under.

Charaka Samhita:

Acharya Charaka says that on account of various aetiological factors, Vata gets vitiated and it fills up the rikta srotas of the body causing various kinds of vatavyadhi, which affects the whole body or some specific part of it (Ch. Chi. 28/18). Besides its self provocating Nidana, vayu is also vitiated by Dhatukshaya and Avarana in Srotasa (Ch. Chi. 28/56).

Various causes leading to Vata Prakopa:

Langhana, Rasakshaya, Rikta srotasa,Vataprakopa, Laghu, ruksha annasevana Atimaithuna, Shukra kshaya, Marmaghata, Margavarana,Vegasandharana, Ama

Vishishta Samprapti:

Charaka Samhita:

Vayu beholds either side – right or left of the body, dries up sira and snayu of that part rendering it dead, along with Ruja and Vakstambha.

Sushruta Samhita:

Excessively agitated Matarishva holds on Adhoga, Urdhvaga and Tiryaka dhamanis, loosens the sandhi bandha of either half of the body and renders it dead (Su. Ni. 1/60-61). Here, Acharya Dalhana comments that Dhamani of only affected half are involved. Here it comes to notice that samprapti described by Sushruta differs from that of Charaka in following two ways.

- Involvement of Dhamani is considered instead of Sira snayu.
- Laxity of sandhi bandha is considered as a part of Samprapti.

Ashtanga Sangraha:

Vagbhata has assimilated samprapti of both Charaka and Sushruta and he says that Vayu hold half of the body, dries up Sira and Snayu, loosens sandhi bandha and leaves either half of the body dead (A. S. Ni. 15/40-42). Here, Vagbhata has considered Sira snayu as a part of Samprapti instead of Dhamanis thus; following Acharya Charaka on the other hand he has also considered laxity of joints as part of this Samprapti following Sushruta.

Madhava Nidana and Bhavaprakahsa:

Madhavakara and Bhavamishra have literally followed Vagbhata in this respect (M. Ni. 22/39-40; B. P. M. Kh. 24/205). Acharya Charaka has described six types of Samprapti, which are described here in context with Pakshaghata.

Sankhya Samprapti: Various types of a disease are considered under this section. There are three types of Pakshaghata as said in Madhava Nidana.

1.   Shuddha Vataja
2.   Pittanubandhi
3.   Kaphanubandhi

Pradhanya Samprapti: This samprapti is described by taking in account the Tara- tama bhava of doshas. Pakshaghata is a Nanatmaja vatavyadhi so, naturally Vata dosha is affected. But even in Vata, the subtypes chiefly affected are Prana vayu, Udana vayu and Vyana vayu. Also, Pitta or Kapha may be associated in Pittanubadhi and Kaphanubandhi Pakshaghata respectively. Pakshaghata which occurs due to its own causes may be taken as svatantra, while that occurring due to other causal factors like tumor, may be considered as paratantra.

Vidhi Samprapti: Vidhi means variety, but as per Gangadhara Vidhi means visheshana. Thus, it may be of two types: Nija and Agantuja, three types depending on dosha and four types depending upon prognosis. Another meaning of Vidhi is onset of disease depending on it there can be two types. One is of sudden Onset and other is of gradual onset. Hemiplegia occurrs due to haemorrhage, embolism is examples of sudden onset, while that occurring due to neoplasm is of gradual onset.

Vikalp Samprapti: This can be taken as Anshansha kalpana. Quality of Vata like Ruksha, Laghu are called as Ansha. In pakshaghata, usually Ruksha and Sheeta guna are increased while Chala guna is decreased.

Bala Samprapti: When Nidana, Purvarupa, Dosha and Dushya are profound in number and strongly involved then disease is said to be of Balavana type and vice versa. Pakshaghata due to fulminating blood pressure along with anaemia and affecting larger area of brain can be considered as Balavana.

Kala Samprapti: Kala Samprapti is understood in context of age of patient, time of occurrence of disease with respect to season, day and night and time of increase or

decrease of disease. Pakshaghata occurring due to CVA usually occurs after 40 years

i.e. Vata prakopaka kala. Hemiplegia due to embolism usually occurs in young age. Hemiplegia due to thrombosis usually occurs in Varsha ritu, last part of the day and night. All these are Vata Prakopaka kala.

Samprapti Ghataka chiefly constitutes Dosha, Dushya, Srotasa, Ama and Agni. Detailed descriptions of each in context of Pakshaghata are as under.

- Dosha - Pradhana Dosha- Vata Prakara -- Prana, Vyana, Udana
- Anubandhi - Pitta, Kapha
- Dushya - Dhatu--- Rasa, Rakta
- Upadhatu - Sira, Snayu,kandara
- Agni - May be affected
- Ama - May be present
- Srotas - Rasa Vaha, Rakta Vaha
- Sroto Dushti - Sangha
- Udhbhava sthana - Pakwashaya
- Sanchara sthana - Dakshina\ Vama Sira, Dhamani, Snayu
- Sthana samshraya - Shiras
- vyaktshana - Ardha Sharira
- Dosha: Pakshaghata chiefly involves Vata dosha. Coming to its subtypes Prana, Udana and Vyana are chiefly involved.
- Dushya: In Pakshaghata Rasa, Rakta, Mamsa, Meda, Sira (Gruhitvad Ardha Shareera Sira snayu vishoshana), Snayu(Sarvanga ekanga rogascha kuryad Snayugato

Anilaha), Dhamani(Adhogamaha satiryaga dhamani urdhva dehaga) and Mala are involved.

- Srotasa: In Pakshaghata Rasavaha, Raktavaha, Mamsavaha and Medovaha srotasa are involved.

- Srotodushti: Atipravritti, Sanga, Sira granthi and Vimargagamana are four types of Srotodusti. All these types are observed in Pakshaghata. Paralysis occurs due to obstruction in cerebral vessels leading to ischaemia. This can be considered as Sanga. Various types of aneurysms can be considered as Siragranthi. Cerebral haemorrhage can be considered as Atipravritti and Vimargagaman.

- Ama: When quantum of Agni is decreased, it leads to production of undigested or semidigested material. This is termed as Ama. This Ama possesses Snigdha, Picchila guna and it causes obstruction in various Srotas. Srotorodha further causes vitiation of dosha. Srotorodha also hampers nutrition of various dhatus leading to dhatukshaya. In pakshaghata Rasagata and Raktagata Ama (Thrombusembolism) are produced, which obstructs cerebral arteries causing ischaemia in brain tissue and leading to its necrosis (dhatukshaya). All these causes Vata prakopa i.e. increase in Ruksha, Shita guna of vayu and decrease in its Chala guna (loss of voluntary movements).

- Agni: All diseases occur due to vitiation of Agni. In Vatavyadhi Agni remains Vishama. So, in Pakshaghata also the Agni remains Vishama.
- Udbhava Sthana : Pakvashaya
- Adhisthana : Ardhsharira

Prakriti as one of Nidana: During the time of Prakriti nirmana Kapha dosha is responsible for Upachita Paripurna Anga, means Kapha dosha is responsible for normal anatomical development. If due to any factors Kapha dosha is vitiated then there would be absence of upachita paripurna anga i.e. Interpretation and incorporation of Ayurvedic principles of aetiopathogenesis along with modern findings in Pakshaghata anatomical anomaly.

We can correlate this anomaly with anomaly of circle of Willis, which is frequently found in patients of stroke. Anatomically compromised circle of Willis is unable to maintain normal blood flow in the brain predisposing the person towards the development of stroke. Dosha: Vata is the chief culprit of this disease. On being vitiated it induces various types of pathology, which prepare the background for hemiplegia. Vata dosha also causes Sankocha, which can be interpreted as follows – Vasospasm is one of the factors that produce cerebral ischaemia. There is evidence that cerebral vessels in animals as well as in man can go into a state of spasm as a result of needling, manipulation and impaction of embolus. We can correlate these factors as under.

Needling -A type of Abhighata, a Swaprakopaka Nidana of Vata. Manipulation --A type of Abhighata, Swaprakopaka Nidana of Vata.

Embolus - A type of Avarana, causing Rikta Srotasa beyond obstruction thus vitiating Vata dosha.

Dushya: Rasa, Rakta, Mamsa, Meda, Sira and Snayu are the Dushya of this disease. Vitiated Vata afflicts the above-mentioned Dushya and induces a nidus necessary for Pakshaghata. Due to excessive Ruksha, Khara type of Ahara, Rasa dhatu becomes devoid of its Snehansha leading to Raukshya of succeeding dhatus as well as Sira and Snayu. Anaemia is described as a potent cause of ischaemia in modern science. Presence of anaemic condition in a person liable for transient ischaemic attacks increases his risk for stroke by manyfolds. Mamsa dhatu is also described as one of Dushya of Pakshaghata. If we consider all three tunics of blood vessels as a representative of Mamsa dhatu then understanding its role in Pakshaghata becomes easy. Excessive indulgence in Vata prakopaka nidana like Ruksha, SheetaAhara-Vihara leads to loss of Snigdhata of this dhatu. This leads to loss of elastic forces in blood vessels making it unable to respond by dilatation or constriction in conditions of hypertension and hypotension. As a result, there is either ischaemia or haemorrhage in the brain both of which can lead to stroke. Meda dhatu is also considered as a dushya of Pakshaghata. We can interpret this in following way. Plugging of vessels by cholesterol is a major cause of ischemia. Also increased levels of LDL with respect to HDL may be considered as a symptom of Dushita Meda dhatu. This causes increased atherosclerosis leading to ischemia.

Sira: Sira is also considered as Dushya of Pakshaghata. Chronic stenosis of either internal carotid or basilar artery produces state of episodic insufficiency in circle of Willis.

Agni: As per Ayurvedic principles each and every disease is directly or indirectly caused due to vitiated Jatharagni. When quantum of this Agni is either increased or decreased it may cause a disturbance in function of Bhootagni and Dhatvagni as well, leading to various diseases. Finding of choleycystokinine, gastrin like hormones of Gastro- intestineal tract in brain gives logical support to the above thinking. The factors or enzymes responsible for dissolution of thrombus/embolus can be correlated with Bhootagni. If these are disturbed then it leads to Pakshaghata.

Ama: Leaky Gut syndrome can occur when toxins, bacteria or incompletely digested food molecules pass into blood stream due to break down of intestinal barrier and can eventually affect brain. The same pathogenesis can occur in hemiplegia also. Ama in a broad sense is any element, which is not completely digested or metabolized, it occurs due to deficiency of enzymatic actions over its substrate. Ama is acquainted with Pichchhila properties and atherosclerosis can be correlated with this. Atherosclerosis plays a lion's share in hemiplegia. Thrombus and embolism can also be categorized under Ama, which are not dissolved by enzymes.

The Physiological Corelation of Mastishka, Majja, Sira Snayu and The Brain:

To identify with the Ayurvedic point or view of the underlying patho-physiology of the disease, it is quite necessary to look upon to the relevant description of the Sira, Snayu, Majja Dhatu and the Mastishka, as well as the Avaraka pattern of provoking Vata. Such pertinent facts denoted in different classics are given herewith: Shira is Sneha Vagbhata, in a metaphoric illustration related Shira (brain) with root of plants and mentioned that as diseases of Shira (brain) attack functional root of human kind, they should be treated as early as possible. Hence Shira is Uttamanga of the body. Majja in the Shira is Mastishka, opined Dalhana and Chakrapani. Sushruta mentioned Parshva Mastishka. Commenting on this observation, Dalhana also noted Paschat Mastishka. He also correlated Mastulunga with congealed Ghrita. Meda is converted into Mastishka and Mastulunga in Shira. Mastishka develops from Prasada part of Asrika and Kapha. Snayu are the functional root of Mamsavaha Srotas.

Mamsa Holds various Sira that carry the Rasa Rakta complex, Snayus and Srotas. Shira is a seat of Indriya-Pranavaha Srotasa.

Here Indriya means various centers present in the brain. Indriyavaha Srotasas are sensory pathways, while Pranavaha Srotasa means motor nerves. Chakrapani commented that these Indriya-Pranavaha Srotasa are all pervasive in the body, however they exist mainly in the Mastishka. This concept clearly illustrates the existence of two open pathways, one from Shira to the body and another from body to the Shira.

There are 900 Snayus in the body and each has its root in Shira (brain). Peripheral nerves may be interpreted as Snayu. Being a Mahamarma, Shira also has roots of all four types of Sira i.e.Vatavaha, Pittavaha, Kaphavaha and Raktavaha deeply embedded in it. Literary meanings of Avarana are obstruction, blocking, closing and covering.

Avarana, as explained by Chakrapani, is Vegapratibandha and Gatihanana. All Avaranas are explained by Shringagrahi Nyaya, defining exactly the involvement of Vata and other Dosha. It is a general rule that the Dosha, which causes Avarana, displays its own symptoms overpowering the symptoms of Vata, being encumbrance to it. Avarana is evident in Pakshaghata. Hence, to cohere with the symptomatology and pathology of Pakshaghata, understanding of Avaranas like Pittavritta Prana, Pittavritta Udana is imperative. This Avritta Vata Dosha, of course, has to settle in Dhatus i.e. Dushya to produce diseases. So, the symptoms of Gata Vata also appear in Pakshaghata. Nevertheless, no single Avarana process covers all symptomatology of Pakshaghata, so the concept of Mishra (mixed) Avarana is pertinent here. Eighty five percent of strokes are caused by cerebral infarction. Formation of a clot in one or more than one cerebral artery is the chief cause of cerebral infarction. There must be a substantial loss (Shoshana) of Dravatva and Snigdhatva to form a clot in blood vessels. This Dravata belongs to Rakta Dhatu, whereas Snigdhata belongs to Meda Dhatu. Sushruta explains the decisive role of Medogata Sneha in the formation of Sira. Siras are Upadhatu of Rakta. Without Vata there will not be any Shosha. The Guna that is responsible for Shoshana is Ruksha. Vishada Guna absorbs Kleda (moisture) and Khara has same qualities as that of Vishada. Thus, Khara, Ruksha and Vishada fractions of Vata Dosha have ability to impart such type of Shoshana to Meda and Rakta.

Charaka clearly mentioned that Khara, Ruksha and Vishada Guna could cause Pakshaghata. Pitta by virtue of its Ushna and Tikshna Guna can lead to Shosha of Dravatva and Snigdhatva of Meda and Rakta respectively. Fire reduces water and it does this more quickly when the wind blows concomitantly. It is the most common example can be given in this regard. Now it is discernible from above discussion that Vata by its Khara, Ruksha and Vishada Guna and Pitta by its Ushna and Tikshna Guna may produce clot/clots in cerebral vessels. In Pakshavadha hoarded Doshas are located in the Mastishka and wreak havoc on it. Prana Vayu Dushti is important In Pakshavadha. Along with

Prana Vayu, Udana and Vyana Vayu are another two to get involved in the pathology.

Harita explained that intensively provoked Pitta, Marut, Shleshma, Udana and Prana get settled in Shira (Brain) and lead to Nashtacheshtata. These elucidations explain the mechanism of how Mastishka regulates all body functions and how vitiated Dosha located merely in Shira can hamper all the movements of the body, which is seen in Pakshaghata. Shiromarmaghata is described in our classics.

Trauma to Sadyapranahara Marma (Shira) commonly manifests in Indriya Artheshu Asamprapti (sensory and motor loss), Mano-Budhhi Viparyaya (deranged mental functions and loss of cognition ability), and a wide variety of severe pains. Shiromarmaghata by Dosha leads to instantaneous death, but if the blow is not that strong; it may result in death after time (7 or >7 days) or major disability or severe pain. These all stages of Shiromarmaghata persist in the patients of Pakshavadha. All patients have one or more than one stage according to severity of blow they receive to the Shiromarma. Even a mild irritation/trauma (by Dosha) to the Marma (Shira) results in a sudden and vigorous activation of Vata throughout the Sira (and Snayus) present in the body. This reckless Vata produces all above-mentioned symptoms with loss of functions of one or either side of the body and the patient lands up in the most common crippling disorder i.e. Pakshaghata. This is a very brisk phenomena, that's why suffix Vadha/ Ghata, which indicates that abruptness is used. Cerebral hemorrhage shows a clear association of Pitta and dominancy of Rakta in its Samprapti. In case cerebral hemorrhage along with Shosha of Sira and Snayus. Sira burst and blood comes out. When Kapha is in the state of diminution then aggravated Vata and Pitta lead to Parishosha (of Sira and Snayus), Sphutana (tears the cerebral vessels) etc. Some scholars consider it as Urdhvaga Raktapitta. The Sira involved in Pakshaghata are Aruna type of Sira.

Sapeksha Nidana

Sapeksha Nidana is very much important for the perfect start of a treatment. Many diseases share common symptoms and it is the duty of the physician to demarcate these resembling diseases. Pakshaghata is primely characterized by loss of voluntary movements. Sapeksha nidana of Pakshaghata in this context with diseases having this symptom is described as below.

Ayurvedic point of view

Pakshaghata and Ardita: All the texts have described these two diseases as separate entities.

Charaka Samhita: We will have a bird's eye view over pathology and symptomatology of these two diseases to understand and differentiate each.

Pakshaghata: Vitiated Vata seizing the vessels, affecting the function of one side of the body and constricting the veins afflicts the right or left side of the body, producing loss of movement, pain and loss of speech.

Ardita: Aggravated Vata affects half of the body, diminishes the blood flow in affected arms, knee and causes contraction of these parts. Either half of the face is distorted or asymmetry of nose, brow, forehead, eye and jaw are produced. Morsel of food doesn't go straight into mouth but instead sideways, nose is curved during speech, eyes do not blink and sneezing is suppressed. Speech becomes indistinct, stutter and thick. Teeth are loosened and there is pain in ears, eyes, temples, cheeks, hand, calves, thighs and feet. This condition whether it occurs along with paralysis of half of the body or alone is called Ardita or facial paralysis.

Here the symptoms like distortion of face, asymmetry of nose, brow, forehead, and eyes are present only in Ardita and not in Pakshaghata. Here, Dradhabala adds that when force of paroxysm is gone in Ardita, patients' returns to normal and if this does not happen then the patient remains afflicted. From this we can infer that unlike Pakshaghata, Ardita occurs in paroxysms.

Chakrapani differentiates Ardita and Pakshaghata by saying that Ardita is associated with Vega whereas Pakshaghata is not. Chakrapani has used the term Ardhanga vyapi Ardita for Ardita and Ardhanga Vata for pakshaghata.

Sushruta Samhita: Describing Ardita, Sushruta says that neck and half of the face are distorted longitudinally and bent. Tremors are experienced in face; speech deteriorates and there is deviation of eyeball. Affected neck, chin and teeth become painful. These symptoms can be correlated with facial paralysis.

Ashtanga Samgraha and Hridaya: In these two texts the description of Pakshaghata and Ardita is similar to that of

Charaka Samhita and hence the points of difference also remain same.

Madhava Nidana: Commentator of Madhava Nidana has used Samanya Ardhanga Vata for Pakshaghata and Vishishta Ardhanga ghata for Ardita.

Modern Review of Pakshaghata and Ardita: Facial paralysis described in Modern Medicine can be correlated with Ardita. In facial paralysis, facial nerve is affected. As a prodromal sign there may be pain behind the ear for previous one or two days after which facial paralysis develops. Pain may be absent. Eyes on the affected side could not be closed and it may water. Mouth is drawn towards opposite side, saliva may drool from angle of mouth and during mastication, and food may collect between teeth and cheek. There is numbness in affected side though there is no apparent loss of sensation. Lines of expression are absent. Patient is unable to close his/her eyes and on attempting to do that it rolls up. This is due to Lower motor neuron lesion in which both voluntary and emotional movements are equally affected in upper as well as lower part of face. Contrary to that hemiplegia is due to upper motor neuron lesion affecting one side of body and only lower part of face. Jaw reflex is slightly exaggerated in hemiplegia whereas it is decreased in facial paralysis. So, Ardita is a variant of Pakshaghata, Ardita is episodic i.e in Ardita one can recovery from neurological deficit completely. Wheras In Pakshaghata there will be permanent neurological deficit or there might be partial recovery.

Pakshaghata and Ekanga Ghata: In Pakshaghata, any one side of body is affected whereas in Ekanga ghata any one of the four limbs is affected. Ekanga ghata can be considered as monoplegia, which occurs due to less space occupying lesion in cortex, on the contrary hemiplegia occurs due to involvement at level of pyramidal tract, involving larger area. Vakstambha is an exclusive symptom found in Pakshaghata, while Hastapada Sankocha and Sirasnayu vishosha may be present in Ekanga ghata.

Pakshaghata and Sarvanga Vata: Sarvanga Vata is characterized by loss of function of whole body. Thus, it is comparable with quadriplegia or double diplegia or cerebral diplegia. There is loss of function of both upper and lower limbs. On the contrary in hemiplegia only one side is affected. In most cases of Pakshaghata, functioning of lower limb recovers and patient is able to walk with little improvement but in Sarvanga Vata the patient is completely bed ridden.

Pakshaghata and Khanja-Pangu: Khanja is characterized by loss of function of anyone lower limb. Patient becomes lame and walks limping. The lesion is in lumbosacral plexus and so wasting is common, which is rare in hemiplegia (if it occurs it may be due to disuse). In hemiplegia the lesion is in pyramidal tract and Involvement of upper limb is usually present. Pangu is characterized by loss of function of both lower extremities. This is comparable with paraplegia. Here also the lesion is essentially in lower motor neuron or other local nerve plexus. There is also loss of control over defecation and micturition, which are usually absent in hemiplegia. Differential diagnosis should also be done between Pittanubandhi and Kaphanubandhi Pakshaghata. In Kaphanubandhi Pakshaghata Shotha, Shaitya and Stambha are present whereas in Pittanubandhi Pakshaghata symptoms of Pitta like Murccha, Daha and Santapa are present.

Sadhya Asadhyatva

Various opinions in this regard in Ayurvedic literatures are as follows –

Charaka Samhita: Pakshaghata has been classified Yatnasadhya (Kashtasadhya) or Asadhya because of the Gambhirya of the Sthana involved (Ch. Chi. 28-73-74). Commenting on word Gambhirya, Chakrapani says that, it means Gambhira sthana Ashraya.

Sushruta Samhita: Pakshaghata cause by shuddha Vata is considered Kashtasadhya, one caused by Samsrushta dosha (Pitta or Kapha) as Sadhya and that caused by Kshaya as Asadhya (Su.Ni. 1/63).

Commenting on word Kshaya Gayadas says that this Kshaya may be of two types-

1. Kshaya caused by excessive bleeding
2. Kshaya caused by excessive exercise like wrestling
    Former type is Asadhya while latter is Kashtasadhya.

Ashtanga Sangraha: Vagbhatta's view differs from Sushruta in this subject. As per him, Pakshaghata caused by Shuddha vata Krucchasadhyatam (Atikrucchasadhya -indu), that caused by samsrushta dosha is Krucchasadhya and that caused by Kshaya is Asadhya (A.S. Ni.15/43).

Madhava Nidana: Madhavakara holds same view as Sushruta but in addition he says that Pakshaghata accompanied by Vedana nasha and those of garbhini, sutika, bala, vruddha, kshina should not be treated. Pakshaghta occurring due to excessive bleeding should also be discarded (M. Ni. 22/43).

Bhavaprakasha: Bhavamishra has followed Sushruta Samhita in this context.

Prognosis depends on the type of stroke, the degree and duration of obstruction or hemorrhage, and the extent of brain tissue death. Most stroke patients experience some permanent disability that may interfere with walking, speech, vision, understanding, reasoning, or memory.

Thrombosis:

Approximately 70% of ischemic stroke patients are able to regain their independence and 10% recover almost completely. Approximately 25% of patients die as a result of the stroke. when focal ischemic lesion is within the territory of the internal carotid artery, the greater the extent of the area of cerebral damage, the worse the outlook. Previous strokes, unconsciousness, association of sensory loss, hemiplegia are bad signs. The longer the delay in onset of recovery, the poorer the prognosis.

Cerebral Embolism:

Cerebral embolism as such is rarely fatal unless the embolus lodges in the internal carotid artery. The immediate mortality of cerebral embolism is 7-10%. Here the eventual prognosis is determined by the progress of the condition causing embolism and the gravity of the underlying illness – cardiac failure, MI, malignant growth, etc.

Cerebral Hemorrhage:

The location of a hemorrhagic stroke is an important factor in the outcome, and this type generally has a worse prognosis than ischemic stroke. A cerebral hemorrhage may prove rapidly fatal. A patient with a pontine hemorrhage or capsular hemorrhage which bursts into one lateral ventricle is unlikely to survive more than a day or two, a progressive hemorrhage in these sites proving fatal by causing brainstem compression. If the hemorrhage is continuing there is a progressive depending of coma, indicated by inability to rouse a formerly responsive patient and loss of corneal and papillary reflexes.

There is no separate description of Upadravas of Pakshaghata in Charaka Samhita, but Upadravas of Avarana are mentioned. They are Hridroga, Vidradhi, Pleeha Roga, Gulma, and Atisara. However, the features mentioned in some of the Anyonyavruta Vata and Anyavruta Vata can be considered as Upadravas of Pakshaghata since the patient are frequently presented with these features like Sarvendriya Shoonyata (Murcha), Smruthi and Balakshaya are present in an unidentified, improperly managed case of Pakshaghata. Features of Shirograha, Uchwasa Nishwasa Sangraha and Mukha Shosha may be seen as Upadrava of Pakshaghata associated with Hridroga in case of Pranavruta Udana. Sushruta has elaborately described eight Maha Roga including Vatavyadhi in general. Specific upadravas of Vata Vyadhi are Shotha, Bhagna, Adhmana, Supta Tvacha, Kampa, etc.

Charakacharya mentioned Swedana, Snehana and Virechana treatment modality for Pakshaghata. Acharya Jejjata & Gangadhara interprets this as Snehayukta Svedana(Sneha Dhara Sweda) and Snehayukta Virechana (with Eranda Taila, Tilwaka Ghrita). Vagbhata acharya described Snehana and Snehayukta Virechana for the treatment of pakshaghata.

So, in the treatment of Paakshaghata one can opt,

- Snehana
- Swedana
- Mrudu Virechana
- Basti
- Nasya

Table No-6- Treatment for Vata Vyadhis-

THERAPY	S.S	C.S	A.S	V.S
Snehana	+	-	+	+
Swedana	+	+	+	+
Virechana	+	+	+	+
Vamana	+	-	+	-
Anuvasana	+	-	+	+
Asthapana	+	-	+	+
Mastishkya	+	-	-	-

Shirobasti	+	-	-	-
Abhyanga	+	-	-	-
Upnaha	+	-	-	-
Yatha-Dosha Samsarga Chikitsa	-	-	+	-
Rasayana	-	-	+	-

Table No-7 Virechana as Treatment for Vata Vyadhi Vis – Pakshaghata

Opinion in different samhitas	Virechana
Charaka samhita	+
Kashyapa Samhita	+
Sushrutha. Samhita	+
Vangasena	+
Astanga Sanghara	+

Snehana (oleation therapy) is a key preparatory and therapeutic procedure in the management of Pakshaghata (hemiplegia) in Ayurveda. It plays a crucial role in balancing Vata dosha, which is the primary dosha involved in the pathogenesis of Pakshaghata.

1. Dosha pacification: Pakshaghata is mainly caused by vitiated Vata dosha. Snehana, being Snigdha (unctuous) and Vata-pacifying, helps calm the aggravated Vata.

2. Improves mobility and reduces stiffness: Snehana helps in softening the body tissues, improving flexibility and reducing the stiffness, dryness, and rigidity seen in hemiplegia.

3. Facilitates better nerve conduction: By nourishing the Majja Dhatu (nervous tissue), it potentially supports neuromuscular rejuvenation and function

Types of Snehana used in Pakshaghata:

A. Abhyanga (External Snehana):
   - Regular oil massage using medicated oils like:
   - Mahanarayana Taila
   - Dhanwantaram Taila
   - Ksheerabala Taila
   - Ashwagandha Bala Lakshadi Taila

Benefits: Improves circulation, relaxes muscles, relieves pain and stiffness, and enhances skin and nerve health.

B. Snehapana (Internal Snehana): Administration of medicated ghee or oil orally (e.g., Maha Tiktaka Ghrita, Ashwagandhadi Ghrita, Kalyanaka Ghrita

Benefits:

It helps to remove Dosha by making Srotosnigdata

Swedana in Pakshaghata

Swedana (Sudation Therapy) is an essential treatment in the management of Pakshaghata (hemiplegia) in Ayurveda. It is used to alleviate the Stambha (stiffness), Gaurava (heaviness), and Shaitya (coldness) caused by Vata vitiation, which are typical symptoms in Pakshaghata.

Importance of Swedana in Pakshaghata:

- Swedana helps by:
- Reducing stiffness and spasticity in affected limbs
- Improving circulation and promoting muscle relaxation
- Enhancing the effectiveness of other therapies (especially after Snehana)
- Facilitating better movement and reducing pain

Types of Swedana Used:

1. Nadi Sweda (Localized Steam Therapy):

- Steam is directed through a pipe to the affected part using medicated decoctions.
- Common herbs: Dashamoola, Nirgundi, Eranda, etc.
- Ideal for localized stiffness or paralysis.

2.   Pinda Sweda (Bolus Fomentation):

- Patra Pinda Sweda (leaf bolus): Using leaves of anti-Vata herbs like Eranda, Nirgundi, Arka.
- Shashtika Shali Pinda Sweda (rice bolus): Nourishing, strength-promoting, good for chronic cases of Pakshaghata with muscle wasting.

3.   Sankara Sweda:

- A combination of various materials (leaves, powders, pulses) tied in a cloth and heated.
- Offers both heat and massage benefits.

4.   Bashpa Sweda (Steam chamber):

- Full-body steam using herbal decoction vapors after Abhyanga.
- Effective when bilateral or generalized symptoms are present.

Basti Chikitsa (Medicated Enema Therapy) is the most important and effective treatment for Pakshaghata (hemiplegia) in Ayurveda, as it directly targets Vata Dosha, which is the primary cause of the disease.

Why Basti in Pakshaghata?

Pakshaghata is a Vata Nanatmaja Vyadhi (disease caused solely by Vata). Among all treatments, Basti is the best for Vata because:

"Vata-sthanam Pakwashayam – Tasmat Basti Vatahara"

(Vata resides in the colon, hence Basti is the best treatment for Vata disorders)

Types of Basti Used in Pakshaghata:

1.   Anuvasana Basti (Oil Enema):
   - Uses medicated oils
   - Nourishing, strengthening, lubricating
   - Given after meals or on alternate days with Niruha
   - Common oils used:
   - Mahanarayana Taila
   - Dhanvantaram Taila
   - Ksheerabala Taila
   - Ashwagandhadi Taila

2. Niruha Basti / Asthapana Basti (Decoction Enema):

- Contains a mixture of herbal decoction (Kashaya), oil, honey, rock salt, and Kalka (herbal paste)
- Given on an empty stomach
- Removes morbid Vata and toxins
- Rejuvenates the nervous system

3. Yoga Basti (Combination):

- A planned schedule (usually 8 or 30 bastis) with alternating Anuvasana and Niruha:
- For example: 8-day schedule: Anuvasana on Day 1, 3, 5, 7, and Niruha on Day 2, 4, 6, 8

Commonly Used Basti Yogas:

- Dashamoola Niruha Basti
- Eranda Moola Kashaya Basti
- Baladi Yapana Basti
- Ashwagandha Taila Anuvasana

Benefits of Basti in Pakshaghata:

- Balances Vata
- Improves motor and sensory functions
- Reduces muscle stiffness, spasticity
- Enhances circulation and nerve regeneration
- Provides Bala (strength) and Snigdhata (unctuousness) to body tissues

Nasya (nasal therapy) is an important Shodhana (purificatory) and Brimhana (nourishing) therapy used in the management of Pakshaghata (hemiplegia), particularly when there is facial paralysis (Ardita), speech difficulty, or involvement of sense organs.

Why Nasya in Pakshaghata?

"Nasa hi shiraso dvaram" – The nose is the gateway to the head.

Since Pakshaghata affects the nervous system, including the brain and cranial nerves, Nasya delivers medicine directly to the head region, balancing Vata dosha in Urdhva Jatrugata (head and neck) areas.

Types of Nasya Useful in Pakshaghata:

1.   Brimhana Nasya (Nourishing Nasya):

- Best for Chronic Pakshaghata with weakness or facial palsy
- Uses medicated oils or ghee
- Commonly used oils:
- Ksheerabala Taila
- Ashwagandha Taila
- Anu Taila
- Shadbindu Taila
- Dose: 6–8 drops per nostril

- Course: 7 or 14 days depending on the patient's strength

2.   Shodhana Nasya (Cleansing Nasya):

- For cases with Kapha obstruction in head, heaviness, or excess secretions
- May use stronger oils like Shirashooladi Taila or Trikatu ghee

3.   Pratimarsha Nasya (Daily gentle Nasya):

- 2–3 drops daily
- Safe for long-term use
- Helps maintain balance of Vata in the head, supports sensory and motor functions

Indications in Pakshaghata:

- Facial deviation
- Speech impairment
- Drooling
- Eye or eyelid weakness
- Nasal stuffiness
- Cognitive or sensory disturbances

Pakshagata is the disorder manifested due to vitiation of vata in association with pitta & kapha in etiopathogenesis – Vatadosha is vitiated due to dietary factors like excessive intake of foods having katu, tikta & kashaya rasa. Vata also vitiated due to excessive strain & stressful conditions of life & irregularities in diet. When vitiated vata attains strength for & external factors, it provocate & interacts with raktadhatu.

The normal functions of sira, snayu & khandara, which are upadhatus of raktadhatu, are impaired due to interaction of rakta with vata. This result in into loss of functions of half of the body.this painful condition is pakshagata. When pitta dosha is also vitiated along with vatadosha, burning sensation, irriation & stroke are the

The most paradoxical thing about treatment of Pakshagata is "Pakshagate Virechanam". Usually, Virechana is the treatment for pittadosha but in this vatavyadhi virechana is more effective than basti, which is the treatment of choice for vatadosha because of the following points.

Pakshavadha is basically a prana vayu vikaar, the natural direction of prana vayu is from above downwards. In virechana this proper direction of pranavayu is achived better than basti.

In pakshavadha upadhatus of rakta i.e. Sira and Kandara vitiated for upadhatu treatment is given for main dhatu and treatment for rakta dhatu is raktamokshana and virechana, therefore viechana is useful in pakshavadha.

Virechana, the main line of treatment cannot be applied in Suddha Vata condition. Virechana is the line of treatment for Vata Vyaadhi condition where Vata is associated with Kapha, Pitta, Rakta and Meda. Highly effectiveness of Virechan in Pakshaaghaata supports the fact that its Samprapti is due to Aavarana of Vaata with Pitta, Rakta, Kapha and Meda.

Pakshagata is also said to be a disease of majjavaha srotas. Majja dhatu and pitta are said to be form same origin 'Ya Eva Pittadharakala sa Eva Majjadhara kala'. Therefore treatment for majja and virechana is best treatment for pitta. Therefore virechana is the treatment of choice in pakshagata.

The adhishthana of Pakshaghata is Indriyayatana (Mastishka). Mastishka is referred as Mustulunga (Ch. Si. 9/101). Dalhana describes the word Mustulunga as Ghritakaram and Mastishka Majja (Su. Sha. 10/42, Dal.) He further describes Mastishka Majja as Majja dhara kala and again says that Majja dhara kala and pitta dhara kala are one and the same. In pitta dhara kala vikriti, Virechana is the best shodhana chikitsa. As Majja dhara kala and pitta dhara kala are same, Virechana may also act well in Majja dhara kala vikriti. So, Virechana can be adopted in case of Pakshaghata.

Kaphandubandhit and Pittanubandhit Pakshaghata have been described in Madhava Nidna. This can be compared with kaphavritta and pittavritta vata respectively. In treatment of both these conditions Virechana has been mentioned (Ch. Chi. 28/184,185,189).

Virechana Karma is a specific process for elimination of pitta dosha (Ch. Su25/40). It also eliminates kapha dosha either associated with pitta dosha or situated in pitta sthana (A.S. Su. 27). Virechana Karma is also said to be capable of mitigating vata dosha. Mridu Sanshodhanaa (Virechana) has been indicated for the treatment of vata dosha. (Ch. Vi. 6/16; A.H. Su. 13/1; Ch. Chi. 28/84). Hence dushti of all the three doshas is checked by this Karma.

In *Pakshaghata* the main *dosha* involved is *vata*. The natural abode of *vata* is *Pakvashaya* (A.H Su. 12/1). In *Pakvashaya gata vata*, *Virechana* is indicated. (Su. Chi. 4/5).

In case of *Sansargaja dosha*, i.e., if *vata* is affected by *pitta* and *kapha* both, then *pitta* should be controlled first (Ch. Chi. 28/188) and for controlling *pitta*, *Virechana* is considered to be best. Hence in *Doshanubandhita Pakshaghata Virechana* can be considered as a treatment.

Vagbhata has mentioned *Mridu Sanshodhanaa* (*Virechana*) in the general line of treatment of *vata* (A.H. Su.13/1), which can also be adopted for *Pakshaghata*.

Mridu Sanshodhanaa has been mentioned in treatment of *Margavarna*. (Ch. Chi. 9/25). Hence in *margavaranjanya Pakshaghata Mridu Sanshodhanaa*, i.e., *Virechana* can be advocated.

Majjavaha sroto dushti takes place in Pakshaghata and in order to combat the morbidity related to Majja, timely shuddhi has been mentioned. (Ch. Su. 28/28). So here Virechana can be taken as a shodhana measure.

If we see the general line of treatment for vata vyadhi given by Acharya Charaka in Chikitsasthana 28th chapter, then after snehana and Swedana, Virechana has been mentioned as main shodhana measure. In the patients contraindicated for Virechana, vasti has been mentioned. Hence Virechana is considered to be treatment of choice in vata vyadhi and so in Pakshaghata.

Virechana Karma possesses the property of purifying the vitiated dhatus (Ka. Si). It has been advised as a treatment in all dhatu dushti janya vikaras, viz., Rakta, Mansa, Meda, Majja, Shukra gata vikaras. (Ch. Su. 28/25) Srotovishuddhi, Impairment of function of Mana, Buddhi Prasadana, impairment of Indriyas encountered in Pakshaghata, sanga type of srotodushti encountered in Pakshaghata are checked by virechana. Virechana imparts strength to the body and stabilizes all the dhatus. Hence useful in dhatukshayajanya Pakshaghata. (Ch. Si. 1/17; Su. Chi. 33/27; A.H. Su. 18/60).

Therefore, by all the above statements it can be concluded that Virechana is the best Shodhana for Pakshaghata.

Shamanaushadhi In Pakshaghata

In Pakshaghata (hemiplegia), after completing Shodhana therapies (like Basti, Nasya, etc.), or in patients who are not fit for Panchakarma, Shamanaushadhi (palliative internal medicines) are prescribed. These Shamana drugs help pacify Vata dosha, support nerve regeneration, and strengthen the muscles and nervous system.

Goals of Shamana Chikitsa in Pakshaghata:

- Pacify Vata dosha
- Improve circulation and neuro-muscular function
- Provide Brimhana (nourishment) to dhatus
- Reduce symptoms like stiffness, weakness, pain, and speech difficulty

Table no.10 - Commonly Used Shamanaushadhi in Pakshaghata:

Medicine	Dose	Indication
Maharasnadi Kashayam	15–20 ml with warm water, twice daily	Pain, stiffness, heaviness
Dashamoola Kwatha	15–20 ml twice daily	General Vata disorder
Ashwagandhadi Churna/ Avaleha	3–5 g with milk	Strengthens muscles, nerves
Bala Churna / Avaleha	3–6 g twice daily	For debilitated patients
Rasnasaptaka Kwatha	15–20 ml twice daily	Vatahara and Brimhana and Rasayana

In Ayurvedic classics, separate pathya apathyas for pakshagata have not been mentioned, as it is one among the vatavyadhis, hence pathya apathyas of vatavyadhis can be taken as that for pakshagata are as follows:

Table no-8

ANNA VARGA	PHALA VARGA	SHAKA VARGA	DUGDA VARGA	MAMSA VARGA	ANYA AHARA GUNAS
Kulattha	Amla rasayukta Phala	Vartaka	Kshira	Gramya	Taila
Maasha	Dadima	Patola	Ghrita,	Anoopa	Tambula
Godhuma	Draksha	Shigru	Kilatam	Audaka	Matsyandika
Raktashali	Jambira	Lashuna	Dhadi kurchika	Jangala	Madhura rasa
Navina Tila	Badara				Amla and Lavana rasa
Purana shalyodana					Snigdha ahara
					Vrusyam

Pathya Vihara:

Sukhoshna Parisheka, Nirvata Sthana, Samvahana, Avagahana, Abhyanga, Brahmacharya, Ushna Pravarana, Agni Aatapa Sevana, Snigdha Ushna Lepa

Apathya Ahara Vihara

All the vata prakopa karanas are to be avoided

Bibliography

1. Caraka Samhita
2. Sushruta Samhita
3. Ashtanga Sangraha
4. Ashtanga Hridaya
5. Madhav Nidana
6. Bhaishjya Ratnavali
7. Bhavaprakash
8. API textbook of Medicine
9. Harrisons Textbook of Medicine
10. K Nishteswar, R Vidyanath, Sahasrayogam
11. Dravyaguna Sangraha by P. V Sharma

www.ingramcontent.com/pod-product-compliance
Lightning Source LLC
Chambersburg PA
CBHW040129150726
48005CB00015B/2423